GU00832868

The Nine Lives
of Algernon

The Nine Lives of Algernon

JOHN ESPEY

Illustrated by
Claire Eder

CAPRA PRESS
SANTA BARBARA

Designed by Maureen Lauran
Typography by Jim Cook / Book Design & Typography

Published by Capra Press
Post Office Box 2068
Santa Barbara, California 93120

This story was first written for Helen Louise and was also enjoyed by Marty and Heather, followed by Alice and Susan, as well as, in their turns, Clara and Jordan. They have all been generous readers and have no objection to the list growing longer. Algernon himself wishes to express special thanks to Jerry Cushman for making his experiences as an astronaut possible.

CONTENTS

FIRST WORDS

Algernon is a cat, and like most animals in stories he came from the bottom of the garden. The first words he could remember came from The Voice. The Voice broke above his head like thunder and said, "He shall be called Algernon." This was a great relief to Algernon, because he had not been certain who he was.

After The Voice had said, "He shall be called Algernon," The Hand picked him up and took him Inside. He had not been in the Garden very long, and for many weeks he could not remember just what it was like. But he always remembered that there had been the Garden.

Sometimes this worried him. Later, when he became a member of the Sons of the First Invasion, he was asked to sign his full name in the book. Luckily, Algernon had thought about this, because The Voice had given him

The Nine Lives of Algernon

only one name. All the other Sons of the First Invasion had at least two names, and some of them had three or even four names. He had a nickname by this time, but he knew it would not be dignified to sign himself "Algernon (Algie)" and to be "Algernon Bottom" did not please him.

When Algie stepped up to sign the book all the other Sons crowded up, waiting to see what he would write. They were sure that he had only one real name and they twisted their whiskers and winked at each other. Algie first wrote down the name that The Voice had given him: "Algernon." Then he paused, looking around at all the other Sons. He knew that they wanted to make him feel uncomfortable, but he smiled to himself and, after dipping the pen in the ink again, he wrote "du Jardin."

This, of course, was after he had studied French, a language that he did not usually speak. All the other Sons had to stop twirling their whiskers because they had not known that his last name was "du Jardin."

At first Algie was blackish grey and small. He learned that when The Voice spoke medium loud he would find some bread and milk in his dish. When he was a little older he got some meat or fish as well. He learned that when The Voice spoke very loud he should stop what he was doing and go to his box. But what he liked most was when The Voice grew soft, because then The Hand would pick him up and hold him and stroke him and scratch him under his chin. When this happened, he would answer The Voice by purring, something he had just learned to do and enjoyed.

Algie became handsome as he grew up. He had bright green eyes and his hair grew long. The upper layer of his hair was almost black, but beneath it was striped. When he became distinguished, his friends often complimented him on having tiger blood in his veins—his enemies said that it was just plain alley and shook their heads. However, they never said this when he was around.

For weeks Algie had no idea that he was to be a distinguished cat. He just lay around eating and sleeping and playing. He might have spent all his Lives like this, except that one day he heard The Voice talking in a most unusual way. He learned later, about the time he was studying French, that this was called poetry.

We now give what Algie heard The Voice saying, because it was the second most important thing in his Lives, the first being when The Voice had said, "He shall be called Algernon."

This time The Voice said:

> Algernon looks with greenish eye
> On each unconscious passer-by.
> Algernon sets small store in words
> But ardently attends on birds,
> Especially when they are seen
> Foolishly pecking at the screen.
> Algernon's a bastard, begging your pardon,
> But I got him myself in the bottom
>   of the garden.
> Now, my dear friends, can you guess after that
> Who Algernon is?
>   He is our cat.

As soon as Algie heard this, he knew that he would be famous. He also knew that the moving things he had been watching through the window were birds. He was not quite sure what some of the words meant, but he felt it was very kind of The Voice to speak of him in this way.

After he had thought about the lines for a long time, Algie decided that he should begin to live his First Life and that he should start it Outside. He waited for a chance and finally he slipped from the Inside to the Outside. To keep from being frightened, Algie kept saying to himself the lines that The Voice had spoken.

I
FIRST LIFE

World Traveler and Explorer

At first Algie was frightened and kept saying the poem over and over to himself. Then, when he found that nothing happened, he stopped saying the poem and looked around him. The sun shone and the air smelled of flowers. The house he had come out of sat on the side of a hill, and the hill, half hidden in bushes and trees, curved away from him. Some birds in the trees squawked at him, but he paid no attention to them because he had to decide what he was going to be in his First Life.

The pleasant smell of the flowers invited him to come and see the hillside. Algie knew then that for his First Life he would be a World Traveler and Explorer, because travel would be broadening and he should see many interesting things.

The Nine Lives of Algernon

He sniffed at a chrysanthemum in the Garden. It made him sneeze. He found a dusty spot on the ground and rolled in it. This was partly a natural thing for him to do, but he also hoped that it would make him look a little older than he really was and would give anyone he met the impression that he was quite an experienced World Traveler and Explorer.

He looked all around him carefully so that he would not forget where he came from. Then he heard The Voice and decided that he should leave quickly.

At first Algie paid little attention to what was around him because he found it was exciting just to run as hard as he could and to climb fences. Then he found that it was easy to run up into trees, though it was harder to get down.

When he was at the top of his third tree and was feeling rather sorry that he had climbed it, Algie paused and began to think.

"This running around is all very well for an ordinary cat," he said to himself, "but if I am going to be a famous cat I must not act so foolishly. I must go slowly through the world and look at things carefully, so that I can be wise and have a good First Life. Then in my Other Lives, when someone asks me if I have smelled the purple asters at dawn in the north, I can say that I have; and I can ask him if he has rolled in the healing dust of the western hills at high noon; and then everyone will know that I have been a successful World Traveler and Explorer."

So Algie climbed down the tree with great dignity and went on with his tour.

A little later, he found a bird's nest in a low bush and

began to make a study of the home-life of birds so that he would know about their habits and would get the true feeling of their life.

While he was doing this, Algie was upset to learn that the birds did not like him to look at them in this way.

"I am only being a World Traveler and Explorer," Algie said politely. "I am trying to understand the life of others."

The Nine Lives of Algernon

He smiled agreeably, but the birds just made a lot of noise and one of them flew down at him and pecked at his ear.

This made Algie angry. He crouched in the grass near the shrub. The next time the bird dived at him, Algie slapped it with a paw, only thinking to teach it better manners. But his claws caught in the bird's feathers and the bird made so much noise that Algie bit it. Then, to his surprise, he found that he was eating the bird and the bird was good.

After he had finished, Algie saw what a fine thing bird-life was. "Birds are very good," he said. After thanking the birds who were left for this lesson, he went on, swishing his tail elegantly and feeling very good inside until he heard someone talking. An old white cat with one blue eye and one green eye was speaking to him, saying, "If I were you, I would turn down the hill here."

"Why?" Algie asked, trying to look experienced.

"Because if you cross this little path, you will get into the yard of the Yellow Bomber," the old white cat said and closed his eyes.

Now Algie could see that this cat was old and wise and knew that Algie was just beginning his Lives. So he stopped pretending that he knew everything and said, "I am very young, but I am going to be famous and I want to learn many things. Right now I am having my First Life as a World Traveler and Explorer. Please tell me why I should not go into the yard of the Yellow Bomber."

The old white cat opened his blue eye and said, "I can see with one eye that you are very young, but you are also very polite. The Yellow Bomber is the best fighter in the world and he kills anyone who goes into his yard. So if you

8

are going to be a famous cat you had better go around the Yellow Bomber's yard."

"I must admit," Algie said, "that I have never heard of the Yellow Bomber. Still, since I am a World Traveler and Explorer I think I should see everything I can."

The old white cat closed his blue eye and opened his green one and said, "You must learn to draw the line." Then he closed his green eye.

"That sounds interesting, though I don't understand it," Algie said. "May I ask what your name is?"

"I was born Reginald Rag-Rug," the old white cat answered. He opened both his eyes and blushed, which looked funny through his white fur. "The younger set call me Old Caution because I have spent all my Lives being a Cautious Cat. I am only in my Fifth Life now, but I am older than most who are near the end of their Ninth."

"Thank you very much for the information," Algie said. He thought the old white cat was something of a bore and began to back away. Without realizing it, he backed right across the little path and into the Yellow Bomber's yard.

The old white cat said, "One down . . ." and Algie was wondering what that meant when he heard a great yell behind him. From the corner of his eye he saw a huge yellow cat with black whiskers leaping towards him.

Algie began to run.

Algie ran as fast as he could, but he could hear the Yellow Bomber close behind him, swearing under his breath. Algie ran harder and harder because he understood now what the old white cat had meant and that his First Life might be cut short any minute.

Algie tore through the grass and brambles. With each

leap the Yellow Bomber gained on him until he could feel the Yellow bomber's breath on the end of his tail.

Then a wonderful thing happened. At first Algie thought it was a miracle. Just as he was trying to fix in his mind what he had learned as a World Traveler and Explorer so that he could remember it in his Other Lives, he saw ahead of him what looked like the Garden. The Yellow Bomber was almost on top of him, but Algie made a last desperate dash for the Inside. The Voice thundered and the Yellow Bomber slowed down. Algie jumped into the Inside.

He was tired and glad to be back. When The Hand fed him, he ate politely. As he ate, he thought very hard and he saw that getting back to the Garden had not been a miracle; for now he knew the truth. He was never surprised in his Other Lives when people spoke of the world as being round. He already knew this and he knew that he had been around the world.

But Algie felt a bit tired of his First Life and decided to try some of his Second Life before he finished his First.

II

SECOND LIFE

Fighter and Cat of Action

Algie stayed Inside for many days. He wasn't at all sure now that he was going to be a famous cat. This upset him, because he didn't feel that any of his Lives would be worth living if he couldn't realize his ambition.

At last he began to think of what he might be during his Second Life. He thought and thought about this, because even though he had been around the world, he felt that the trip hadn't been a complete success.

The more he thought about it, the more he saw that what made him unhappy was the Yellow Bomber. "If I could only get rid of the Yellow Bomber," he said to himself, "I could move right along and be a famous cat."

Just saying this didn't get rid of the Yellow Bomber, so

at last Algie understood that the only way out was to become a Fighter and Cat of Action.

Though Algie was a handsome cat, he wasn't as big as the Yellow Bomber. He ate as much as he could, and he tried to get foods with many vitamins in them. He liked to eat, but instead of becoming big and strong he just got fat and heavy. He knew he didn't exercise enough, so he went out to the Garden and did push-ups. Even with this, he knew that he didn't begin to equal the Yellow Bomber.

One day, though, he remembered the old saying: *The Brain is Keener than the Claw,* and working from this he knew he must plan a campaign.

His first step was to get a little experience, so he went Outside one night and was careful not to let anyone know he was around until he found a cat just half as big as he was.

He walked up to this cat and said, "I am Algernon and I am learning to be a Fighter and Cat of Action. Wouldn't you like a practice fight?"

Algie had crouched down low so that the other cat would not see how big he was. Instead of answering politely, the other cat let out a big yell and jumped at Algie. In this way Algie learned the value of a surprise attack.

The other cat turned out to be just as big as Algie, and while the two of them clawed at each other Algie thought that he wasn't going to like being a Fighter and Cat of Action. He was about ready to give up and turned over on his back. He had very long back legs, and now he found out how useful they could be.

The Nine Lives of Algernon

The other cat, when he saw that Algie had rolled over on his back, got ready to come in and finish him off. But as the other cat jumped, Algie kicked out desperately with his long back legs. One foot tore the other cat's face and the other caught his left ear and ripped it.

The other cat screeched and said, "Quits! I give up."

Algie got up and dusted himself off and said, "Thank you very much for your cooperation. Please speak when spoken to the next time."

"Yes, sir," the other cat said.

"Good-night, then," Algie said and walked away. He was happy to be called "sir," and he felt again that he was going to be a famous cat. He felt proud of his long back legs and from time to time he stopped and stretched first one and then the other, learning just the right moment to put out his claws.

The next few nights, Algie tried out his fighting technique on a number of cats and he learned many of the fine points of being a Fighter and Cat of Action. He learned to make ugly faces and terrible noises, and he found out that, although you can be polite before and after a fight, you should forget your manners while you are really fighting.

After these bouts, Algie rested for a few days. Then he said to himself, "Now I am ready for the Yellow Bomber." And that night he went out to meet him.

Algie felt fine and strong. As he went towards the Yellow Bomber's yard he sang a little song to himself:

> I'm going to bomb the Yellow Bomber,
> I will rip his ears.

He will holler
for his mommer,
And I don't care if she hears.

Algie felt so happy that he made a small chorus to go with his song:

All my joy and my distraction
Is to be a Cat of Action.

Algie was singing this so beautifully that he almost forgot to speak to the old white cat with one blue eye and one green eye. Algie saw him just in time.

The old white cat opened his blue eye and said, "Excuse my looking at you this way, but are you feeling quite all right?"

"All my joy and my distraction is to be a Cat of Action," Algie chanted. "I must go now, but I'll be seeing you soon."

"The pace young people live at nowadays!" said the old white cat, closing both eyes. "Nice to have known you."

Algie crossed the path and went into the Yellow Bomber's yard, pretending he couldn't see him crouched behind a bush.

When the Yellow Bomber jumped out, Algie saw that he was very big. But he remembered his plan, and anyway he wasn't going to run away in front of the old white cat.

Algie played as if he didn't see the Yellow Bomber leaping towards him until the very last second. Then he squeaked and rolled over on his back.

The Yellow Bomber laughed out loud and began to

pounce on Algie. Algie hit out with his long back legs and one foot tore the Yellow Bomber's face as the other caught the Yellow bomber's left ear and ripped it half way off.

The Yellow Bomber was really in very poor shape because no one had dared to fight him for a long time. He shouted, "Quits! I give up."

Algie got up, dusted himself off, and said, "I am Algernon, and I am going to be a famous cat. Right now I am being a Fighter and Cat of Action."

"Yes, sir," said the Yellow Bomber.

"Now I want you to go and tell the other cats that I have beaten you," Algie said. "From now on, anyone who wants to can play in your yard."

"Yes, sir," the Yellow Bomber said. He went off and told the other cats that Algie had beaten him. When the other cats looked at his face and his ear, they believed him, and the old white cat told the same story.

Algie became very well known. He was called Cat of Action Number One, and some spoke of him as "Socko Algie," and for a while he felt quite happy.

But no one would fight with him any more, so it was hard for him to go on being a Fighter and Cat of Action.

So one day when Algie went home he felt tired of his Second Life and decided to try some of his Third Life before he finished his Second.

III
THIRD LIFE

Major Lover and Casanova Cat

Algie was really a friendly cat, so it hurt him to think that everyone was afraid of him. Whenever he wanted to strike up a casual conversation, all anyone would say to him was "Yes, sir," respectfully and then look for the quickest way to leave.

So when Algie decided to start in on his Third Life he turned around and made up his mind that he would become a Major Lover and Casanova Cat.

Algie did his best to make himself handsome, and for two or three days he exercised his singing voice, hoping to become even more attractive and dashing. The Voice itself didn't seem to like Algie's singing very much.

When Algie could trill without difficulty and hold a note for a full minute and then go up and down the scale three times, all in one breath, he felt that he was ready to start out on his Third Life.

The Nine Lives of Algernon

Many cats were doing their best to be Casanova Cats, so Algie was able to watch and see how to become one. After he had watched for a while he said to himself, "All these fellows use the same sort of line, and that is why they have so much trouble getting anyone to go out with them. It would be silly for me to do the same old thing."

What Algie had noticed was that everyone trying to be a Major Lover and Casanova Cat sang just about the same sort of song, sounding like this:

> I am a very lonely cat,
> Singing all alone.
> I really cannot think that
> Anyone could like this moan.
>> Then please be good enough to stop my sigh,
>> O-h m-e, o-o-h m-y-y,
>> Ho-ow very sad a-am I-I!

> I know how beautiful you are,
> You are much too good for me,
> You are like a flowery star,
> And I am just a hungry bee.
>> Then please be good enough to stop my sigh,
>> O-o-h m-e-e, o-o-o-h m-y-y-y,
>> Ho-o-ow very s-a-d a-a-am I-I-I!!

"That is a silly song," Algie said. "It hasn't a good rhythm and the tune is monotonous. I will make a better song."

So Algie made a better song with a good rhythm and some pleasant variations from major to minor. The first

night he went out to be a Major Lover and Casanova Cat
he sang:

Solomon was not as wise
As the wisdom in my eyes,
   My beautiful green eyes.

Poor man, he had a thousand wives,
What a lot of Private Lives:
   I'd rather have the hives.

I have been around the world,
   I turned it in one day.
My tail is naturally curled,
   I brought the Yellow Bomb to bay.

19

The Nine Lives of Algernon

> I really do not think, dear ladies,
> > You are good enough for me.
> It's hardly worth, poor Sals and Sadies,
> > Your time to come and see.
>
> For I'm a most intelligent cat,
> A splendid and an elegant cat,
> > A clearly sheer superior cat,
> > And a very very good,
> > Oh a very very good,
> An excellently good posterior cat!

When the other cats trying to be Major Lovers heard Algie singing this song they laughed. They knew that this was not a regular cat love song. But all the young lady cats felt excited and came to look at Algie.

He strolled up and down in front of them, singing his song. At the end of each stanza he swished his tail and took a pinch of catnip snuff. He pretended not to notice that all the young ladies were watching him and growing more and more excited.

But at last Algie stopped in front of the prettiest young lady and said, "You're not half bad—not bad at all. Come along with me." The prettiest young lady felt flattered and went along with him.

After this, Algie had all the young ladies at his feet, in a manner of speaking. If he liked one of them especially well, he let her call him Algie, just as we have been calling him that all along for convenience. People spoke of him as a Major Major Lover, and when he was mentioned in the gossip columns he was called "Casanova Algernon."

Algie enjoyed all of this, but after a while he grew sleepy and tired and almost a trifle bored. He knew all the young ladies and he felt that he had done as much Major Loving and Casanova Catting as he was up to for the present. And one morning, as he drifted home, he realized that he was a bit weary of his Third Life and he decided to try some of his Fourth Life before he finished his Third.

IV
FOURTH LIFE

Simple Hermit

It isn't easy to say much about Algie's Fourth Life. Just as he had turned right around after trying out his Second Life and had become the opposite for his Third, now he turned right around from trying his Third Life and became the opposite for his Fourth. The odd thing was that he didn't go back to his Second Life, however. This shows that he was getting older and wiser, because the opposite of a thing often changes.

Algie decided to rest up and be a Simple Hermit for his Fourth Life, and that is where the trouble of telling about it comes in. A Simple Hermit spends all his time alone and he talks to no one but himself. Even then, he usually doesn't use words that anyone else can understand, but the language he uses instead of ordinary words is more important to him than regular sentences. Just a few wispy ideas like "full circle" or "Conservative Christian Anarchist" are often more important to a Simple Hermit than complete statements.

So Algie spent part of his Fourth Life being a Simple Hermit on top of the hill. He sat there all day, reading a little and thinking a little.

Algie took up the study of the French language, which was later to be so useful to him. He liked the French language very much and he thought of himself as *Le Chat Solitaire,* and sometimes he sat for hours saying *"Je suis tout seul"* to himself. This was the same thing as saying "I am all alone," but it seemed to mean something quite different when he said it in the French langauge.

At other times Algie would sit there and think to himself, "I am Algernon. It is I who am Algie, and Algernon is I, Algie, and me." Then he would brood over the philosophy of grammar.

Often a number of the other cats would gather at a respectful distance and watch Algie. No one spoke to him, because it is not polite to speak to a Simple Hermit. But they would say to each other, "Algie is a very faithful Simple Hermit. Do you think he will ever stop?"

Whereupon, the old white cat would say, "Most of them do."

The young ladies felt sorry that Algie had become a Simple Hermit, but even they admired him for it. It had been a long time since anyone had been a Simple Hermit for one of his Lives.

After a while Algie began to feel the disadvantages of being a Simple Hermit. He didn't speak to anyone and no one spoke to him, so he couldn't tell if he was still on his way to becoming famous or not.

And so one day, when he was especially tired of being a Simple Hermit, Algie left the top of the hill early and went home and decided to try at least a bit of his Fifth Life before he finished his Fourth.

V
FIFTH LIFE

Big Business Cat and Monopolizer

When it came time for Algie to decide what he was going to be in his Fifth Life, he realized that his would be his Middle Life, and he wanted to be sure that he chose the right thing.

"I have gone into some of my other Lives a bit hastily," he thought to himself. "For my Middle Life I must choose something sure to help me become a famous cat. I must find out what people say they most respect in Lives and be that."

Algie went out and soon learned that the richest cats were the most respected cats. So he decided that for his Middle Life he would be a Big Business Cat and Monopolizer.

Algie had always remembered how good his first bird on the wing tasted, and knew how much all the other cats liked fresh bird on the wing. Often this was hard to get. A cat could waste a whole day trying to catch a bird.

So Algie went to the birds and spoke to them politely. "I have come to talk over a Big Business Proposition with you," he said. "I have noticed that there are birds that are outlaws whom you won't allow to live with you."

The birds, twittering from a safe distance in the trees, agreed with this.

"Well," Algie went on, "I want you to sign a contract with me so that all those birds will be turned over to me and to me only. If you will do this, I will see to it that no cats hunt any of the good birds; and I will distribute the Criminal Birds among the cats. This is what is known as a Big Business Proposition."

The birds discussed this proposal for a long time and were suspicious at first. But finally they decided to give Algie the Criminal Monopoly on a trial basis.

Algie went out and announced to all the other cats that he had a private Criminal Bird Monopoly and that only he was to deliver birds to the cats. He reminded them that he hadn't finished his life of being Cat of Action Number One. The birds would turn over all their criminals to him under the terms of the Criminal Monopoly and he would sell them to the other cats. From time to time, he sent out circulars telling how much better tasting and racier Criminal Birds were than Good Birds.

This proved to be a satisfactory arrangement. Algie grew richer and richer until he was the richest cat around.

It was at this time that he became a member of The Sons of the First Invasion, almost the highest honor that could be awarded, and this proved that Algie was an

important cat. The only trouble was that no one knew if he really ought to belong, because he didn't know anything about his father.

But the old white cat solved this difficulty. "After all," he said, "Algie behaves just like a Son of the First Invasion, and only a Son of the First Invasion behaves the way Algie does. Therefore, or *ergo,* he *is* a Son of the First Invasion. Besides, he may reduce his price to members."

All the other Sons agreed and elected Algie by a voice vote.

For a while he felt that he had done everything he could to become a famous cat and he felt satisfied.

Then he started to have trouble. Some of the cats objected to his prices and began to catch Good Birds on the sly. The birds complained to Algie. He tried to find out who the cats were, but nobody seemed to know for sure.

The birds refused to deliver as many criminals as they had before. Algie's supply ran low, and this made many of the cats angry. They came and sat on the picket fence around the Garden and said Algie was not fair to them. Algie had to hire some very low-class and disreputable cats to run through the line on the fence and carry on his business for him.

Things kept getting worse and Algie saw that he might lose some money. So he sold his Monopoly at auction and put all his profits into Government Bonds, even though the rate of interest was low.

The cat who bought the Monopoly couldn't make a new agreement with the birds. He came to Algie and asked for his money back.

Algie said, "My money is all in Government Bonds now, and to get any back would upset the National Balance. I am very sorry. Goodbye."

With his Monopoly gone and his money safe in Government Bonds, Algie grew tired of being a Big Business Cat and Monopolizer and decided to try a bit of his Sixth Life before he finished his Fifth.

VI
SIXTH LIFE

Orthodox Economist

A fter Algie had retired for the time being from Big Business he had no trouble making up his mind about what he was going to be next. He had been proud of his idea of a Private Monopoly. Even if it hadn't worked quite as he had expected in the end, he felt that his theory was sound and he thought that other people should be interested in it.

So for his Sixth Life Algie became an Orthodox Economist, which sounds much harder than it really is.

All Algie had to do was make up a lot of ideas that didn't need to fit anything, and then ask people to pay to listen to him talk about the ideas. Even though what he said never seemed to do them much good, all the other cats thought Algie's theories were very significant. Only a short time after he had started to be an Orthodox Economist, everyone was repeating his remarks.

The Nine Lives of Algernon

These remarks often sounded a little silly, but no one seemed to notice that. Algie would say, "Demand supply," and then he would say, "Supply demand," and then he would say, "That makes a Big Business Cycle."

The other cats nodded and paid him money. Then they would go back to their Little Businesses and would say to each other, in a sort of chant, "Demand supply, supply demand, let's have a Big Business Cycle." This didn't make any difference in their Little Businesses, except that they were a little poorer because they had paid Algie to tell them his ideas.

Algie talked and talked. Since he said the same things over and over again, and the other cats paid him over and over again to say the same things, there isn't much sense in repeating what he said here.

He might have gone on this way for a long time if he hadn't grown so fond of hearing himself talk. "It's a great pity," he thought to himself one day, "that all I can talk about is the economy, because I know so many other things as well. In fact, I know so much that sometimes I feel like singing about it or making up a few rhymes as decoration."

But when he tried to talk about other things or sing a stanza or two or even introduce a pithy couplet to make a point, the cats grew angry and refused to pay him. "He is an Orthodox Economist," they complained to each other,

31

"and he hasn't any right to talk about anything more interesting. And who ever heard of any kind of Economist talking in anything but prose?"

So Algie had to go back to giving his standard talks. He lost a little face over this, and some of the other cats went around behind his back, saying, "Algie was getting too big for his claws."

One day Algie overheard a cat saying this around behind his back and he went home feeling sad. "I haven't many more Lives to experiment on," he thought to himself, "but I really don't want to go on being an Orthodox Economist."

He thought about this and grew sadder and sadder. He kept hearing himself singing and making up rhymes and finally he decided to try a bit of his Seventh Life before he finished his Sixth.

VII

SEVENTH LIFE

Major Poet with Three Periods

Algie had come to enjoy singing to himself and making words into patterns so much that for his Seventh Life he decided to be a Major Poet with Three Periods.

He had another special reason for doing this. His Third Life love song had become so successful that many other cats had gotten into the habit of using it. This made Algie angry, so he decided to publish it. Then it would be copyrighted, and before any other cat could use it he would have to pay Algie some money.

Algie wrote and wrote. Finally, for his First Period, which was his Yes Period, he brought out a book of poems called *Rooted Green*. Algie's love song and many other poems were printed in this book. One of the others shows what this poetry was like:

The Nine Lives of Algernon

ALIVE

What other cats have written
Of weeping sadness
Is not for me—I am not smitten
With such madness.

I love the whole wide world,
The hill and flowers;
In sunshine I lie curled
Outside: Inside during showers.

Why should you or I be sad
With so much to see?
We should all be very glad
And happy just to be.

The other cats read *Rooted Green* and said, "He is young and talented and shows great promise."

So Algie wrote and wrote a lot more for his Second Period, which was his No Period, to avoid monotony. Finally, he brought out his second book, which he called *Nadders and Pads*, a pleasingly bitter phrase meaning "Snakes and Toads" that he had found in *The Peterborough Chronicle* when he was being a Simple Hermit.

The Nine Lives of Algernon

This second book was quite different from the first. This is the sort of thing it had in it:

PLASTIC HEART

No beat can pass
transparent veins unseen
lest pulsing weariness
transgress the whispered sign.
No longer stand
no longer wait the horn
for feeble tremors end
in a long slow burn.

A sonnet (which is too long to give here) beginning "Give me the pastel of some lesser god," became popular.

Near the end of this book, Algie grew very bitter, as in this poem:

THE PRICE OF LIFE

Pennies for gas
Pennies in the slot of doom
Pennies for sighs for a gay alas
Pennies perhaps
Will last until bed and collapse.

Algie didn't think much of this book and wrote it only because he was being a Major Poet with Three Periods and knew he had to have a No Period. But the other cats read *Nadders and Pads* and said, "He is bitter and acute and shows great promise." Algie wrote and wrote a lot more for his Third Period, which was his Greater Yes or Ah! Period. He called his third book *Wedded Brick*. Here is the most famous poem in it:

QUI SAIT?

Now the world before me lies
Quietly beneath my eyes,
Good and bad are clearly shown,
The eternal dice are thrown.

Yet with one eye good is good,
And with the other good is bad;
And with the first eye bad is good,
And with the second bad is bad:
I cannot tell which eye I should
Believe, egad!

The cats who read *Wedded Brick* said, "He has made a synthesis and is now a Major Poet with Three Periods ..."

Although you might think that Algie had now finished his Life as a Major Poet with Three Periods, this was not so. A Major Poet with Three Periods can go right on writing for a long time, and occasionally may even write some poems that are not half bad.

But Algie had grown tired of writing poetry for the time being, so he decided to try a bit of his Eighth Life before he finished his Seventh.

VIII
EIGHTH LIFE

Space Scientist and Astronaut

Before he chose his Eighth Life, Algie decided that he should consult public opinion, so he went to see the old white cat.

"I have been so busy living my Lives," Algie said to him, "that I haven't kept up with everything that is going on nowadays."

"That's true," the old white cat said. "What's more, you've been very impulsive all the way along."

"At least I've enjoyed myself," Algie said.

"I suppose," the old white cat answered. "But we have moved into a new world while you've been enjoying yourself."

"A new world?" Algie asked in surprise. "It looks pretty much the same as ever to me, begging your pardon."

"Granted," the old white cat said. "But it isn't. We are now living in a new world of space science."

"So you think I should become a scientist, whatever that is?" asked Algie.

"No, you are getting on too far for that," the old white cat said. "I have noticed that truly great scientists get their one truly great idea quite early—in their First, or, at the most, Second Life. Then they live on their reputations for having had that one great idea and move on to be Public Figures, or Administrators, or even Advisers to the President."

"What a bore!" Algie exclaimed. "But I do wish you had told me about this earlier."

"You never took the time to ask," the old white cat said. "Anyway, I don't think you were cut out for that. But there is still one way you might become a kind of scientist, really a space scientist."

"How is that?"

"Thank you for asking," the old white cat said. "You could volunteer to be an astronaut."

"You mean actually travel through space?" Algie asked.

"Exactly. I've heard that the beings who run the Space Program are called NASAns and want to find out how intelligent individuals like ourselves would behave during a trip through space."

"That's interesting," Algie said. "Thank you for your advice."

"Don't mention it," the old white cat said.

Algie went to NASA, only half-believing what the old white cat had told him. To his surprise, the NASAns grew excited when Algie volunteered to be a Space Scientist and Astronaut.

"You're exactly what we've been hunting for," the

NASAns said, "a creature who can obey our orders and show how certain levels of life will react in orbit."

"In orbit?" Algie asked.

"Yes, in orbit," the NASAns said. "You go up into outer space and then orbit round and round the Earth."

"That's interesting," Algie said politely, thinking to himself that it sounded silly and that he had better not let the NASAns know that he had already been around the world several Lives before.

So Algie found himself going through some strenuous training, whirling around in small spaces and learning to function in a small globe for hours at a time. Some of this was tiresome, but Algie stuck at it because he learned that no one had ever heard of a cat being a Space Scientist and Astronaut before and he knew he would be scoring a first-time triumph.

At last the day came when Algie rocketed up into space and found himself alone in his own globe as it went into orbit. He could look out of a window and see the world as he circled it. From time to time the NASAns asked him over the radio to pull certain levers or punch certain buttons or turn on the TV camera to take pictures of himself and of the Earth.

Each time he did one of these simple chores the NASAns would praise him. "Great work, Algie!" they would say. "Isn't it amazing what Algie is able to do all by himself?"

Algie thought that even a moderately intelligent dog could, if carefully trained, carry out these jobs and felt a little bit disappointed. But he did enjoy looking at the

EIGHTH LIFE

Earth, though its size surprised him. Thinking of his first journey around the world made him homesick, but he said nothing about that to the NASAns and kept on doing what they asked him to, boring as it all was.

After three days Algie had run through all the experiments possible and the NASAns brought him out of orbit. He was excited by the sense of speed he felt before the landing, but he hadn't expected to be greeted with so much excitement.

"You were terrific, sir," the NASAns told him. "We must work out a more sophisticated routine for your next flight."

"Thank you very much," Algie said politely. "Take your time. It got rather boring up there. I think I'll postpone the rest of my Astronaut Life for a while and try something else."

He stepped out of the NASAns' building and was astonished by the cheering crowd that greeted him.

"Whatever you say, sir," one of the NASAns said.

"Thank you," Algie said, "but why have you started to call me 'sir'?"

"We were afraid it might distract you while you were in orbit," the NASAn said, "but while you were up there you were made a colonel in the Air Force."

"I was?" Algie asked. "I never noticed the difference."

"Well, you may notice it now, sir," the NASAn said. "But no matter what you do, sir, please keep in touch. We are already planning your future flights. You must realize, sir, that you have already put us far ahead of our competition."

"I guess more has gone on than I realized," Algie replied

modestly as he waved to the cheering crowd. "Don't worry, you can always reach me at home."

After waving to everyone Algie got into the special car reserved for him and asked the sergeant to drive him to the hill so that he could save the rest of his Eighth Life and think about what he might try for his Ninth Life.

IX
NINTH LIFE

Philosopher

I have done a lot of fooling around," Algie said to himself, "and a lot of studying, and a lot of talking, and a lot of writing, and a good bit of thinking. Now I am going to do a lot of thinking." So, for his Ninth and Last Life, Algie decided to be a Philosopher.

All the other cats were impressed by this. Algie was already a famous and distinguished cat. Now that he was going to be a Philosopher, he would probably be one of the most distinguished cats that had ever lived. He might even be made a member of The Order of The Sphinx.

Now, it is not very difficult to be a Philosopher, though it sounds hard, and many Philosophers like to pretend that it is very hard indeed. But all you have to do is sit and think and get ideas to fit with what you are thinking. So

Algie thought and got ideas, and he sat some more and thought some more and got some more ideas.

Then Algie noticed a funny thing. When he sat and thought with his eyes open, looking at what was going on

around him, he would make one kind of philosophy. But when he sat and thought with his eyes shut, not looking at what was going on around him, he would make a different kind of philosophy. He worried about this, because he knew that a Philosopher should make just one System, and here he was making two Systems at the same time.

Finally he hit upon a solution. He would make part of his System with his eyes open, and then he would shut his eyes for the same length of time and make the next part of his System. Then he would open his eyes again and make some more of his System, and then he would shut them again and make still more of his System.

This worked out very well, and at last Algie announced that he was making what would be known as the Open and Shut System of Philosophy.

Everyone was impressed.

The other cats waited for Algie to give them his Conclusion, but for many days Algie said nothing more to anyone. He just went on making his System.

After he had made his announcement, Algie became a member of The Order of The Sphinx. No one knew quite how this happened, but one morning someone said, "Algie is now a member of The Order of The Sphinx," and this turned out to be true.

After a few more days, Algie finished The Open and Shut System of Philosophy. He spoke at last to the other cats, saying, "Tomorrow I will give my Last Words or Conclusion."

The cats who heard him say this went far and wide,

telling everyone they could find that on the next day Algie would give his Last Words or Conclusion.

That night, Algie felt very happy. He had reached a splendid Conclusion. And all that night the other cats kept coming in from miles around so that they could hear the Last Words or Conclusion of Algernon, which will be the climax of this story.

LAST WORDS

The morning of the day that Algie was to give his Conclusion, all the other cats began to gather early on the hill. Many of them had come from a great distance and had brought their breakfasts and lunches with them. When they arrived they sat down and ate their breakfasts and began to wait.

Everyone wondered what Algie's Conclusion would be. The oldest cats there remembered having heard one or two other cats who had been Philosophers, but could not recall their Conclusions. The old white cat could remember, though not word for word, three Conclusions. All these Conclusions had been very long and had taken at least three hours to give. So when Algie did not appear by ten o'clock everyone grew fretful.

The Nine Lives of Algernon

A space on the top of the hill had been reserved for Algie. Around this space, but at a respectful distance, the other cats arranged themselves. First there were The Sons of the First Invasion, who were very proud, because Algie was also a Son of the First Invasion. Then behind The Sons of the First Invasion sat The Invaded Daughters. Most of them had been young ladies when Algie was enjoying his Third Life, so they, too, were very proud.

Behind these two circles sat the other cats according to age and rank and where they came from. Away out on the edges of the crowd, almost at the bottom of the hill, sat the low-class and disreputable cats, for even they had come to hear Algie's Conclusion.

By noon, the cats had all grown restless and some of them were close to being angry. But just when the sun stood directly overhead, a shout rose from the edge of the crowd.

Algie had arrived.

Around his neck hung The Order of The Sphinx, a Nile-green silk ribbon with gold clasps holding a small sphinx made from the immortal delta sands. Algie had curled his whiskers. His coat shone. He held his tail at a delicate angle as he walked, and the slight breeze caught the long hairs in it and waved them daintily.

The other cats drew back in front of Algie, clearing a way to the space at the top of the hill. He walked up, neither fast nor slow, The Order of The Sphinx swinging grandly.

When Algie reached the top of the hill, he paused and made four bows to the crowd, one bow to each major point of the compass. Then he sat down on his long back legs, facing the most distinguished Sons of the First Invasion, who had the most beautiful Invaded Daughters directly behind them.

The entire hillside, crowded with cats, made no sound.

Algie cleared his throat.

At last, in a voice that broke like thunder, he said: "These are my Last Words and this is my Conclusion, reached through The Open and Shut System of Philosophy."

He paused. Then, in a voice even clearer and louder than before, a voice that was like a double clap of thunder, Algie said: "IT IS GOOD TO LIVE ALL NINE LIVES AT ONCE."

After he had said this, Algie bowed deeply and walked home.

All the other cats gasped, not quite sure what Algie had meant by such a short Conclusion.

But Algie himself felt very happy. For, as you have no doubt noticed, Algie had never finished any of his Nine Lives, so he had something left over from each one of them.

The Nine Lives of Algernon

From this time on, Algie has lived all Nine Lives at once. He does some traveling, and a little demonstration fighting (just to keep in shape). He may go out for an evening with a beautiful young lady or he may be a Simple Hermit for a brief period. When he sees the chance for a quick killing he plays the market. Occasionally he writes a poem and publishes it in an expensive limited edition. When NASA can find no adequate substitute for him he generously goes into orbit. He always likes to eat and sleep and think. Every morning he repeats to himself the Conclusion of The Open and Shut System of Philosophy because it pleases him.

Living this way, Algie never uses up any of his Lives because no one can be sure of just which Life he is living since he does everything at once. And if anyone doesn't believe this, all that person needs to do is go to the house on the hill and look at Algie, who is as lively and wise and distinguished and famous today as he was when he first gave his Conclusion to The Open and Shut System of Philosophy:

IT IS GOOD TO LIVE ALL NINE LIVES AT ONCE.